ARRIVAL AND DEPARTURE

ACKNOWLEDGEMENTS

My thanks to anthologies, journals, and magazines where several of these poems were previously published: *Dust & Fire, Encore, Ephrastia, Lakes Region Review, The Moccasin, Moon Reader, Poets' Forum, SIMUL, Talking Stick, Zumbrota Artist Collaboration.*

I thank Five Wings Arts Council for the grant that allowed me to write and market this manuscript. The Five Wings Arts Council is funded by the McKnight Foundation.

PUBLISHED BY:

201 West Laurel Street
Brainerd, MN 56401
www.riverplacepress.com
218.851.4843

Designed and produced by Chip and Jean Borkenhagen

Printed in the United States at Bang Printing, Brainerd, MN.

Author Photo: Randy Stengel

ISBN 978-0-9903563-0-1

To teachers who inspired me

To Rez who set my poetry free

Now & Then: Imagining History

Arrival & Departure

VOCABULARIOS

ECHOES OF GRIEF

NOW & THEN:
IMAGINING HISTORY

HOMAGE
To Lucille Clifton 1936-2010

The stories of your struggles
to become a writer, a poet, haunt me.

You saw your father take
the poems your mother wrote,
throw them into a cookstove fire
and slam the lid on her dreams.
No man nor stove could quench your fire.

I admired your marching on the barriers,
tearing down fences, defying
father, racism, sexism.
Refusing to give in you rose
to become a university teacher.

Recently I shared your poem
"Homage to My Hips"
with Girl Scouts too young to know
the meaning of 'homage', too young
to have hips. I asked them to write poems
about strong things, like hips.

Your hips are wide, wide as ships
that brought your foremothers from Africa.
The caftan you wear camouflages
the dimensions of your hips.
Yet, you celebrate those hips.
Your hips that were never 'enslaved.'

The last time I saw you at Dodge Festival
you needed assistance to mount the stage,
but at the microphone your voice
was strong as a Montgomery boycott.
Your face was black as oil,
your hair white as a slave-holder's arms.
Your un-burned poems burned my ears,
and fueled my resolve to write
with the strength of your black hips.

SACAJAWEA

They call me Bird Woman
a bird without wings
in bondage   as are all women
Stolen from my people
slave to the Mandan
wife of Charbonneau
bound to this little man
strapped to my back
only my mind flies free

Great excitement in the village
when pale-skinned men arrive
a big dog and two chieftains
They wait out winter in our earth lodges
tell stories of the Great White Father
in far-off Washington   He sent them
to explore the land of my fathers

I listen as I serve buffalo stew
My heart swells within me
like springtime willow buds
They learn I traveled
these mountains many moons ago
they bargain with Charbonneau
he trades me for coins and firewater

When the river swallows the ice
we begin the upstream journey
With Pompey at my breast
I turn toward the setting sun
and high meadows of my people

The sinews of our trails
lace together the moccasin
of this walking-forward country

LITTLE CROW: DAKOTA CHIEF

A second son, Little Crow was not meant to be chief. His mother
knew better. She plunged this baby into icy water, rubbed his skin
with snow, sent him into the forest to embrace solitude. His Dakota
name meant His People are Red. He followed the seasons, hunted
deer and muskrat, ever more aware of white man encroaching.

> white men—oak leaves
> in yonder forests—
> or locusts

Little Crow listened to his father and grandfather, chiefs before him.
They counseled, "We must adapt. We must learn to share the land."
But the whites brought disease and whisky and defiled their women.

> under a hot moon
> mad dogs bite shadows
> gnaw at teepees.

In Great White Father's house in Washington, Little Crow signs
papers. Money and food for his people will be sent soon. In
Minnesota winter snow deep as deer belly, cold makes all water
hard as iron. Old people and children die of hunger and disease.
Warehouses hold food. White man will not give it out. Anger
the only heat in deer skin teepees. Promised gold not come.

> arrows flew
> lead answered
> next day, gold came

PICKETT'S CHARGE

They come across that pasture, wide
as all their nights and all their days.
They march in rank, gray surging tide
in woolen suits in summers' blaze.

A friendly place where cattle graze.
They come across that pasture wide-
eyed, this unlike the other frays,
old Pickett's charge damn suicide.

A mile wide no place to hide,
each man keeps marching, each man prays.
They come across that pasture wide
as Hades in a blood red haze

of sweat and fear and war time craze.
When muscles fail they march on pride
as Yankee cannons hold their gaze
they come across that pasture wide.

LONE RANGER COULD TELL 'EM

Kids at the Saturday matinees.
thought riding a horse was exciting.
I could tell them about saddle sores
and hemorrhoids, but
they wouldn't believe me.

I'm glad I was popular before
'political correctness'
shot the hell out of Westerns.
In my day cowboys were heroes
for shooting Indians off ponies.
Faces daubed with war paint
terrorized kids before they
themselves started getting tattoos
that scare the snot out of me.

Did they wonder how we started fires
surrounded by cactus and rocks
nary a match to be seen.
And those bedrolls looked cool
but weren't warm and killed my back.

Life was comfortable in theater seats,
the outcome predictable and satisfying
except for Native American kids.
If all else failed the cavalry rode in
and kids actually stood up and cheered.

My side kick didn't know
that Tonto means "stupid" in Spanish.
And I just found out that "kemo sabe"
translates as "old know-nothing."
Actually only Silver had an honorable name.

WE LAY A PRESIDENT DOWN

Forsake the world's debates
Lay down the power gavel

We wrap you in the flag

Lie down among the flowers
Lie down near honor guard

We shelter you with sacred song

Black horse with booted stirrup
Black blossoming umbrellas

We citizens salute your passing train

Your gift of laughter gone
Your golden tongue is stilled

The country joins to rock you in its arms

Soup Diplomacy

Chef Jared's soup stirs up in us a hunger
to mix herbs, blend chicken with noodle,
beer with cheese, to simmer them to perfection.

Or is the beauty of soup, that time is not its essence.
Potato and leek naturally cohabitate, ugly oxtail
transforms into broth delight. Left-overs
in the fridge resurrect in an other-worldly body.

In the global soup tureen there are no territorial wars.
Oh, occasionally a tomato may curdle its milky broth,
but a tactful cook can negotiate this rift.

We envy Jared's skills persuading nations of tastes
to agree, so those who sup may forswear war forever.

THE MEAL THAT LASTS
The Last Supper, Leonardo da Vinci 1452 -1519

We arrive in Milano the day the exhibit reopens. Art experts had spent
21 years restoring the painting. Students, smug-full of knowledge, we
wait in herded groups inside thick cloister walls. Twentieth Century
technology electronically cleanses us of dust and pollutants. We walk
pure as saints into the huge refectory where monks once ate in silence,
and some practical Father Superior ordered a door cut through the end
wall. Providing more direct access to the kitchen, even though Christ's
feet were cut off under the hanging tablecloth. Below those wounded
feet we stand, stunned by the size of the scene, smitten by colors. Our
guide points out the twelve grouped in trios around the One centered in
solitude. Their gesturing hands seem to ask, "Is it I, Lord?" Each knows
full well it could be he. These walls hold echoes of Napoleon's soldiers
using them for target practice, walls later leveled by Allied bombs. A
sandbag miracle saved the frescoed holy diners. We back away fixated on
the depth of da Vinci's room and the meal that lasts and lasts despite
poor plaster and musket balls. Despite betrayal.

The Inkeeper's Lament

Nothing much happens here
in this little town, off the beaten path.
Our only claim to fame
native son, King David.

I can't complain, my small inn
provides a comfortable living.
We get the Passover overflow.
The pilgrims stop here.

Those gentile Romans
generated the latest bonanza.
This census enrollment
filled every room,
filled my pocket with gold,
and ruined my reputation.

I could see the problem,
that young woman's condition.
Her husband's pleas touched my heart.
I gave them shelter,
and their donkey, too.
What did it get me?
An uproar of shepherds
and bad press.

I am remembered
for two words.
No room.

WEDDING AT CANA

The rabbi is late.
The cantor has laryngitis.
Lilies have begun to wilt.
Yet, under a canopy,
the symbolic goblet is crushed.

Each wedding has disasters,
hopefully out of sight—
hopefully guests remain
ignorant or distracted.

Truth be told, most do not care,
so long as it is not their wedding.
So when the wine runs out
they are distracted and ignorant.

Scurrying begins, finger pointing.
Servants try to distance
themselves from the problem.
Until someone's mother rescues
the day with her assurance,
"My son can help."

Her son bids servants
fill large stone jars with water.
The wine steward puzzles over
why the host kept best wine for last.

In the other room celebration continues.
Laughter overflows, cups are refilled.
The guests leave behind empty urns
and a miracle they never knew.

Understanding

Their hands fly as they talk,
conversation heated and excited.
They've come for answers,
or to see a miracle or two.

Word spread through Galilee,
through all Judea about this prophet,
this man who teaches with stories,
stories of shepherds and lost sheep,
of sowers and seeds, of salt
and leavening and light.

Could he be the One, the Messiah?
Would he drive out the hated Romans?
Or at least drive out a demon or two?

As they sit on the arid hillside,
he stands to speak.
He says they are blessed:
blessed in their poverty,
in their sorrow,
blessed in their neediness,
in their hunger,
blessed to be persecuted.

They walk away shaking heads.
Easy for him to talk. He's young.
What does he know of hardship?
He's just a carpenter's son.
He only understands
wood and nails.

Arrival & Departure

I drive with my father to the small town where my grandfather
settled when he arrived in America over a century ago.

>   farmland black as coal
>   banked on the grate of freedom
>   warmth for newcomers

Here among other German immigrants he practiced his craft
of carpentry, cupboards and chests carved with twining vines,
polished to buttery hue. Builder of coffins, he buried the dead.

>   far away from home
>   no familiar forests
>   grass   horizons   grass

My uncle was the only son to remain in this fertile landscape.
Now we travel to visit him as his health fails. He a short man
beside my father's height. Both speak terse male love.

>   sailing overhead
>   gentle breath of death catches
>   dry leaves in tree tops

Hands in pockets they stand and talk. Not saying the things
they both know. Behind them the stacked rock garden, my aunt's
pride. Uncle already looks past us at horizons we cannot see.

>   hard background of rock
>   plans caught in the crevices
>   future under stone

BEHIND THE SCREEN

Eight times three royal women
birthed boy babies for the dynasty.
Joy took flight on origami wings.

Closeted behind silk screen
grand matriarch,
prized mother of three sons,
honored grandmother of eight boys,
inscrutably folds secret hopes
inside her peony red kimono.
At temple she lights joss sticks,
bows extremely low,
quenches unworthy thoughts.

In the courtyard concubines
peer over fans, their dark eyes
tinged with green. They try
to rub against her lucky haunch,
to steal her power.

When I, the least of daughters-in-law
on birthing stool bring forth a girl,
the other wives sigh with relief,
smirk with wicked glee.

Tears on my cheeks
dry like lotus blossoms
when regally grand matriarch
bends low and whispers in my ear,
a daughter—at last!

WAKE FOR A PIANO

The piano died when my son left home.
Proof is in the dust on the cherrywood lid,
the dumb "e" above middle "c".

When he was young, if called for chores
or homework, he hid inside sonatinas.
While he played my dusting had tempo,
the iron glissandoed over shirts,
the cakes I baked crescendoed.

When his older brother took lessons
he wanted me to sit next to him,
to count, to listen to labored fingering,
eager to be done.

Not this second son whose hands
fell naturally into raised curved position.
—solitude and sonatinas—
He played until walls vibrated
and the mailman stopped to listen.

If he ever practiced the assignment,
who knows. The story of his life.
Never octave predictable, he scorned
the simple scores. For him the challenge
of Mozart, the intricacies of Sondheim.

His parents sing below his staff,
cannot climb the scales he conquers,
amazed at this music they spawned,
this artistry he sets loose.

Now no one plays the piano.
The space could hold a love seat.
We know he will not return.
But I cannot sell the piano,
sonatinas still linger inside,
trembling.

EDISON ESTATE, FT. MYERS, FLORIDA

While Thomas Alva spent his days inside
the dark confines of laboratory shed
devising things plain folks would then deride,
"He'll have to show us that it works!" they said.

His light bulb, phonograph and thousand more
inventions proved the man a genius.
In winter on Caloosahatchie shore
his wife was busy too, without much fuss.

She changed the view from her veranda. So
the grassy swamp bloomed under Mina's hand.
A paradise of jacaranda, snow
white orchids, banyan boughs transformed the land.

Tourists marvel at his mental powers,
find cool peace and charm amid her flowers.

Riding the Poetry Horse
"The Circus Rider" Marc Chagall 1887

On the back of a circus-red horse
a white-faced clown
balances on one leg.

In ballerina pose
calico tights stretched thin,
the clown stares cock-eyed,
intent on a steadier future.

In the background
a cherubim, naked as sin,
prepares to break
the predestined fall.

And above all,
in a blue-ink sky,
crowned by beech branches

the necessary moon
pulls tides and pens
across slippery pages.

ARRIVAL & DEPARTURE

OVERTURE

Seated in fifth row of the Kennedy Center
I am gripped by images of a little boy,
dark head bent over keyboard.
I am transported to our rec room
for untold amateurish performances
staged by him and his siblings

When the baton comes up
it is in my son's hand.
I see only the back of his head,
the hair thinning in one spot.
As the music swells
so does my heart.

He the most sensitive child, yet,
most defiant, testing his father's patience.
I standing, like Moses, in the breech
bridging their anger

Now we parents sit, fingers entwined,
as the overture of *Crazy for You*
washes over us in lilting, lusty notes.
The curtain opens, the house lights dim.
Our son has the production under control.
I clear my eyes and see the magic.

AH, JANUARY

Heavy-footed January edges on to the stage
after lights, camera and action are done,
after gifts, eggnog, and Good Will to men.

December, the star, whisked on her way
signing autographs, ending another successful run,
leaving in her wake the unpaid Visa bills.

January looks out on a snowy set
no longer deep and crisp and even,
deeper, crustier, more than slightly soiled.

Cold theater, questionable script,
thirty-one days of rehearsing,
all practice, no clapping audience.

Worst of all, that little slip of an ingénue,
February, waits in the wings in miniskirt,
giggling promises of hearts and chocolates.

ADVICE ON PRAYING

I say when you pray
be bold!
Step up to the plate,
swing with mighty muscle,
swing from the heels.

I believe God
enjoys a good game,
an athletic pray-er.

Forget those mealy-mouthed
"Justs" that imply
you'd be satisfied with less.

One never wants 'just.'
One wants the sky
and wings.

LONG SENTENCE

When I received the letter I was confused because I didn't know anyone in federal prison at least didn't think I did, and the return address was the name of someone I didn't know; I opened it anyway to find a plea from someone named Travis, seeking information about writing poetry, this Travis admitted he was in prison for holding up a drugstore with a gun while on drugs; he did not know anyone else in this prison who was guilty, but that is neither here nor there, the trick was to help the guy learn how to write poetry; my friends cautioned me about having a relationship with a felon, but I told them I was old and "what the hell, by the time he gets out of prison I'd probably be dead, and how dangerous could somebody be who actually *wanted* to write poetry," but I could not mail any books to him unless they came directly from a bookstore, so I asked a friend who owns a bookstore to mail him Kim Addonizio's book "Ordinary Genius" said I'd pay for two books so I could have my own copy to compare passages he might not understand, but obviously he understood the book because the next poem he sent had improved exponentially and I am getting serious about reading my own copy.

FIELDS OF CHILDHOOD

The field of flowering flax
stitched a blue ruffle on the edge
of a section of awned wheat,
a handkerchief of delight
against the golden coin of the realm.
Oats and barley glowed a dusky ocher.

In springtime it was hard to tell
the difference from the backseat
of a dusty Chevrolet, on our customary
Sunday drive, yet my father could tell.
He knew what was planted
when first leaf pushed
through the black Dakota soil.
Shades of green no mystery to him.

My father knew most everything.
I'd heard his stories:
how he survived a motherless childhood,
how he took to the streets at fourteen,
rode boxcars with hobos,
and when hungry and afraid,
winos pressed nickels into his hand.

The land had been reliable, like the seasons,
until one year the crops he planted
sprouted only to die of drought
and record heat drove him out.
Sending wife and children by train,
he followed with furniture in a truck.

A west coast job paid only enough
to pay rent on the "company house."
"If I am going to starve to death,
I'll do it in North Dakota," he swore
as he reloaded the truck
made his way back east,
state by state, job by job,
relative to relative.

Back home on familiar soil
he scraped together and borrowed,
enough to buy a grocery store.
He generously 'carried' farmers
and other folks down and out.
No family would go hungry
while there was food on his shelves.

No wonder each Sunday after church
we would drive out to praise the fields.

Portrait of Madge

On the wall above your head
that minx Madge still flirts
with her portrait painter, your Uncle Kai.
The gilded maple frame fills
one wall of this small room.

Before coming to this 'home'
Madge hung in a place of honor
on your living room wall.
After your husband died
you became fiercely protective,
fearing intruders and thieves.

So Madge moved with you to this place.
She a St. Paul socialite of the 1930s,
sits serenely, her long-fingered hands
lie forever still on her golden silk lap..
Confidently, she dominates the space,
assured her beauty will never die.

Now the priest intones prayers and Last Rites.
Your heart finds it hard to break
its hundred year habit, learn how to
give up the spirit, leave this frail body.
Today you must release this prized
possession, must release Madge
along with jewelry, clothing, books.

While above your head, Madge
gazes out the window from her
place of honor on this dying room wall.

WEDDING MARCH

THE GROOM	THE BRIDE

Stands waiting, braced at his back
by friends, brothers

Comes forward, led by
practiced step of friends, sisters

Armored in resolve he teeters
on shore of uncharted seas

Listing toward her father's
safe harbor she stumbles

Breath strained, he leans
forward, longs for her touch

Pulse in her throat flutters
like a frightened dove

Organ music, cloy of roses
faces of her family unnerve him

Passing her aunts and uncles
backs of his relatives, she falters

He wants to be ten again
up in a tree, somewhere else

She wishes the dress was pretend
flowers plastic, in her bedroom

He spies her white-dressed hope,
breath refills his empty chest

She sees his dark suited devotion,
his dear solid form

His eyes find hers

Her eyes find his

And all the dawns of all the days
And all the stars of all the nights

ALMOST SPRING

His head bald, fringed with gray,
she, daughter-in-law, just past full bloom,
in tandem they bend and rake leaves
and twigs browned by winter,
intent on uncovering the cold soil
of a bed thirsting for sun and seed.
They chat as they gather remnants
of last summer and fall.
Here and there they find the nub
of a bulb anxious for air.
They lift and loosen clods of dirt.
His shoulders permanently stooped,
on her cheek a smear
where she chased a wayward curl.
Unseasonably warm, they know
it is too early for seeds,
snow will fall again
before true spring.
It is not yet April.
But this task is about shared hope
and sweat and two whose roots
are entwined, not by birth,
but by seeds and seasons.

THIS IS MY LOVE
Painted by Leslie Emory

plowing and seeding
seasons slipping through fingers
years circled in gold

The painting above our piano, a furniture store purchase, has been there so long that I can't remember when it came to live with us. I do not remember when this old couple first looked out at us in our long-married wisdom. Although there are no rings in evidence it is obvious they are married.

dovetailed together
cedar chest full of linens
table set for two

His blue eyes twinkle beneath bushy brows and snowy hair. His shoulders proudly squared, his work shirt buttoned to the chin, pants secured by suspenders. One arm rests on her small shoulders, her hand laid across his other hand, as though he has asked her to dance. Dressed in her best black dress, the white dimity collar is crumpled. If she knew, she would ask him to straighten it. He doe not notice. Her black hair is streaked with white. Her eyes gaze far away, perhaps remembering the early years.

a green wind sings hymns
aprons, overalls, diapers
clothesline of history

In the background a mostly cloudy sky with sun seeping through here and there and behind his shoulder we see the edge of a field. A crop not quite ripe or ready for harvest. Void of buildings. No clutter. Just these two rooted to this soil.

tested by nature
drought, flood, grasshopper, cyclone
unbent cottonwoods

How comfortably we have lived with this quiet couple as they stood watch over our long married years. As they looked down on our child-rearing. At our disagreements. Our loving. I wonder what they would write about us.

TAKE ME OUT TO THE CROWD

Baseball's allure may be in its symmetry—
grass mowed cross-hatch,
a measured square cornered with bases,
an elusive white sphere
and a wand waving at possibilities.
The simplicity of one-two-three.

Oh, say do you see
the democracy of the crowd
standing with caps clasped over hearts.
Banker and butcher side by side.
A jovial community of bratwurst,
beer and peanuts passed hand to hand,
money passed back to vendor.

Here the crowd votes loudly
for the team of their choice.
No violence or blood.
The civilized pace creates
a smug contentedness,
the sense that being here
is somehow patriotic,
that hours spent here
are justified and hallowed.

PENANCE

My husband has only four fingers on one hand. Actually three fingers and a thumb. An accident I assure you, even though it is his ring finger that is cut short. I think this is the reason for his dialing wrong numbers. Although it may be because he only has one eye. When I married him he was a complete set. Since then he has managed to leave a trail of body parts behind. In the past, dialing wrong numbers was hardly a mortal sin, not even a venial one. When no one was at home it didn't matter. That was before Caller ID. Now are the days when one's sins find one out. Strangers call me wondering why I called. We sleuth through digits reversed, inverted, scrambled. Courteously I apologize for the transgressions of my husband's errant fingers. However, when he comes through the door, I drop him to his two good knees with penance of three Hail Marys and two Our Fathers.

Time Traveling

Leaving our Minnesota winter,
we fly west, dropping hours
like stitches in my knitting.

Landing, we lean forward
in our seats embracing thoughts
of daughter and grandchildren,
who stand outside SECURITY,
their un-scanned bodies
not yet allowed to touch ours.

We meet them at the carousel
pick up the weight of luggage,
their hugs welcoming us to
Seattle's mild, moist February.

We left home after early breakfast
and arrive here in time for breakfast.
Moving in a time-capsule world–
In our day a thing of science fiction,
an accepted reality to these children
who shrug off the intricacies of time
as casually as a hand knit scarf.

A week later we fly east toward home
and pick up those dropped stitches,
a tedious task of retrieval:
snow to shovel, grocery lists,
appointments grabbing at our ankles,
the calendar pulling us to the tarmac.

The weight of winter wool
lands heavy on our shoulders.

VENICE, SANTA MARIA DELLA SALUTE FROM SAN GIORGIO
Louis Eugene Boudin,   Oil on Canvas

Venice floats on a mirror of lapis lazuli,
an aging courtesan lifting
lacy petticoats above the tide,
her nippled domes suckle the sky.

Henna-rusted roofs hide her graying roots.
Masted boats, sails battened-down,
snuggle against her soft loins,
trading salt and spices for her favors.

Along the canals, gondolas skitter,
proud-necked atop the teal-green water
like black lacquered dragonflies,
regal heads carved with the doge's sign.

Indolent in Mediterranean sun,
campaniles thrust toward milky clouds.
Siesta-time shadows seek cooler depths,
slide under curves of slender craft.

Inside *pensiones* tourists fan themselves,
await evening freshness, uncorking
blown glass bottles. And *Bella Venezia*
pours out her secrets *con amore.*

LOOKING BACK ON NORWAY

The plane crescendos
lifting us above this land
of trolls and stave churches.
Inside us a fjord sings
green glacial notes
and Trollstigen's sharp
switch-backs trill a high C
of hair-raising memory.
Folksongs echo
across snug valleys
hung with grass-roofed
grace notes.
A fugue of roads,
skinny as fish bone,
twists through mountains.
We nose into clouds
thick as curdled cream,
satisfied as barn cats
purring a Grieg melody.

FRIARY RUINS
Ardfert, Ireland

Rough rock arches above my head,
stones placed here centuries ago.
Franciscan brothers in brown robes
once walked along this passageway
palms pressed together,
thumbs and fingers pointed heavenward.

As I walk this ruined edifice
I strain to catch echoes
of the tens of thousands of prayers
that swirled and caught in cracks,
and blessed this place.

Who knows what threw
these men face down
on this stony transept
in cross-shaped vows,
forswearing any issue
their manhood sealed
within these tombed walls.

Young men suffering love's rejection
or escaping uniform and killing,
or sent by parents needing
fewer mouths at their table.

VOCABULARIOS

Planting Tulips with Tom Cruise

He is shorter than I expected.
The Big Screen tells lies in many ways.
But the smile is as advertised,
a thousand watts of teeth.

I kneel at his feet,
my garden gloves claw the soil.
He drives a spade into the bed.
The bulbs lie near my elbow.
I must place them
into the ten-inch-deep holes.
In my nervousness
I keep forgetting which end is up.
Tom smiles encouragingly
which flusters me more.

Here he is, Top Gun,
grounded in my yard.
I want to ask about his wife,
about the Italian wedding.
I want to say something witty.
My lips refuse to move.

His jaw, square as a box office,
shades my head.
He opens another dark cave,
I drop in another bulb.
Slower, slower, I want to cry.
Don't hurry, stay longer.

The bulbs have all been planted.
He turns to leave,
those broad shoulders departing,
that cocky walk taking him away.
I cry out!
Tulips—tulips—two-lips.

ON HEARING THE POET LAUREATE

Billy Collins slouches to the microphone,
balding and not beautiful,
until he reads,
then his words satisfy
like cherry nut ice cream,
his verbs wave tall and proud—
red, white and blue.

His poems skip merrily
across the page,
at times, belly laughing,
at times, slipping on a rueful tear.

It's like a trip
in our Plymouth station wagon
with three kids and a dog,
a chaos of sounds,
a carload of love.

In the New Jersey autumn air
he revives poetry,
spins out lines like saltwater taffy,
puts verses on roller skates,
and we hang on to his belt for the ride,
caught up in a benevolent
hurricane of poetry.

ROGER THE NOUN

She adored him as a noun,
the subject of her sentences,
object of her prepositions,
a conjunction in her life.
She could dangle him like a participle,
Rogering him like a gerund.

At times, like all husbands,
he was an exclamation,
very rarely an adverb.
He was a noun so long
he turned pro,
the genuine article.

They were married forty years
when he decided to be a verb.

She erased him.

SPANISH LESSONS—CHA, CHA, CHA

Spanish verbs dance in my mouth,
bailaring across my mind
in hip-swiveling rumba rhythm.
¡Dudo! ¡Dudo! I doubt
I shall ever learn these complicated steps.

The bouncing *habanera* of adverbs,
slides *lentamente*, slowly over the tongue
in multitudinous syllables—
more amusing than that
simple English step "-ly -ly"
Los adjetivos meekly trail after nouns
follow in winding conga line,
always agreeing with their leader.

Shy *vocabulario*, sexually inhibited,
glides by—¡Ah, you women!
¡Oh, you men!—never neutral.
Dresses, *vestidos*, are male.
Neckties, *corbatas*, are female.
Whoever heard of such things?

Las preposiciones leap into every
sentence, stamping & clapping,
stepping on toes, tripping me up—
a, de, con, por, para—
I do not know if I am *with*,
or *at*, or *for*. I just keep dancing.

The *yo* of I and *tu* of you tango by
cheek to cheek, familiar *pronombres*,
but their kinfolk—
te & *me* & *se* & *le* & *lo*—
keep cutting in. I can't keep
the relatives straight.

¡Las preguntas, las preguntas!
Questions, questions.
I click my *castanets*,
flick open my fan and fandango.
Cry ¡*Caramba*! and stomp my heels.

Ironing Shirts with Bill Clinton

I can't explain how I got the job,
how I came to this place, this man.
Lord knows, I was not a contributor
to his reelection campaign.
One might say we are on opposite sides
of the fence and I want to keep it that way.

Ironing shirts is not difficult,
only time consuming.
Steam heat is essential for getting
all the wrinkles out.

Bill leans his heavy thighs close,
breathing steam of his own.
I catch him with an elbow
as I whip the shirt off the board,
flatten the collar before addressing the body.

I feel a moment of simpatico for Bill,
hanging around the house with the dog,
his wife off to work, too busy to iron shirts,
daughter's wedding over
he can eat cheeseburgers again.

Bill learns quickly.
I hand him an iron.
I am surprised at his dexterity,
his deft finger work.
I set up another board.
We begin to stroke shirts in tandem,
steaming, turning, pressing hard.
We finish the last 2 shirts in unison,
rest our irons on their flat bottoms.
I smile. He smiles. I can sense him moving on,
ready to conquer the next challenge.

I leave, shaking my head,
a strange work assignment,
but better than a desk job.

INTRODUCING THE POET LAUREATE

The man named to introduce
the lady chosen to introduce
the U. S. Poet Laureate,
does not introduce himself.
He consumes my patience
with long minutes of laud
and long lists of credits,
not for the Laureate,
but for the introducer lady.

She steps to the microphone
and in her academic superiority
exalts all of her own insights,
her own accomplishments,
driving me mad with the withholding.

Until, at last,
the small, tanned man,
wispy, white hair floating
above benevolent gnome smile,
fills my waiting sack
with fine-milled Nebraska wheat.
He feeds my hunger
with a harvest of delight,
a meal worth the waiting.

SIMPLY VINCENT
Edna St. Vincent Millay February 22, 1892 – October 18, 1950

No more back and forthing.
No more riding on the ferry.
I lie under sumac for I am very tired.

No more choices,
no more prizes,
no more platforms,
no more apples, no more pears,
no more warring with Mama.

Life was very merry,
but I had grown weary.
No escaping death
of people who matter.
Dear Eugen, who wed my poetry,
allowed me to burn my candle
as I saw fit. Perhaps
he should have reined me in.
I broke our brittle vows
with abandon and panache.
Lovely boys and toys,
lovely pills and liquor,
lately lost their luster.

I am emptied at last of sonnets,
and old age would not become me.
Let my flaming hair go gray?
Nay, I choose the stairway.
Regrets? Oh yes, I have regrets.
But life was very merry.
I rode it to a fare-thee-well,
I cast a lovely light.

It was I who wrote
"Tranquility at length when autumn comes."
So I rest here under sumac.
No more riding on the ferry.

ENTERTAINING INTERLUDE

A Norwegian folk tune glides liltingly,
up the daisy-sprinkled wallpaper,
drifts above the smørgasbord table,
above the pickled herring, above the rommegrøt.

Humming, she tugs a wayward blonde strand
moves the bowl of stewed prunes
beside the plate of cucumbers and tomatoes.
She steps back to survey her Martha Stewart display.

The guests will be here soon—his boss, his friends.
They will fox-trot in, trade Cole Porter banter,
attack her masterpiece with clumsy, atonal fingers.

She wants to pull down a lacy curtain of eighth notes,
to protect her heart-shaped cookies
She wants to wrap her majestic lefse in the
marching meter of Grieg's *"Hall of the Mountain King."*

The doorbell's jarring crescendo intrudes.
She smoothes her apron, lowers the drawbridge,
welcomes the guests with a Billygoat Gruff grin.

A Jar of Coins

The money ran out in the second semester.
Her tuition paid, dormitory as well,
but not her meals, her paper and ink.

She remembers the painful sight
of her father digging up the jar.
He did not know she saw him,
saw him slowly count out
the money coin by coin
with thick, chapped fingers,
mumbling numbers, shaking his head.

Next day he drove her
to the small teachers' college.
He carried the one heavy suitcase,
pulled out a leather pouch,
pressed it into her hand.
"For the t'ings you need," he said
in his Norwegian up-tilted voice.
No hug. No kiss. He left.

Now there were no more coins,
nowhere to get any.

She walked past the sign twice,
a lettered notice in a dusty window.
WANTED: ARTIST MODELS
She understood what was wanted,
her body, naked, exposed
to art students   women and men.
Her heart thundered.
Her hands grew clammy.

On the third day she went in.

When the sheet fell away
her mind painted papa's wheat field
in rolling waves of ocher gold.
With greens she painted mama's garden,

fat cabbage, ferny carrot tops
mother's dark shadow hoeing,
shoulders aching, like her own.

Papa was standing on the platform
the day the train brought her home.
She pressed her teacher's certificate
into his hard hand. He held it.
She knew he could not read.
He looked anxiously into her eyes.
"You had enough?" "Yes, Papa,
you gave me everything I needed."

July Heat Wave

This torrid spell has out-foxed us.
We who had fantasized all winter
about this hot lady
are exhausted by her fans
and her fandango.

There is no sex.
We wake each morning
wanting our good old girl back,
the one who frosts windows,
only to find *this* one
crouched at the foot of the bed
tangled in sheets kicked aside
in the stifling night.

The lawn is a dry crackle
torched by her match,
by her lack of cool.

The dog slumps legs sprawled
on the vinyl floor.
His panting amplifies
her presence, that in-heat
bitch of summer.

ODE TO OLIVE OIL

I know what makes one a virgin,
but what makes one extra-virgin?

I was a virgin (to what age
I need not confess) but I do not believe
I ever reached that "extra" status.

I remember my virgin days
when eager young fingers
fondled virgin oil, temps ran high.
Let me tell you, we cooked,
simmered, boiled and boiled over,
but no smoke alarms went off.

According to the cookbook
the extra-V stuff smokes easily,
making it unsuitable for cooking.
While it is the most expensive,
"used raw a little goes a long way."
Obviously not "all the way" or
it wouldn't be virgin anymore.

Good old regular virgin oil
"stands up well to heat
and is much cheaper."
That line hooked my husband.

Viktor Reads Poetry

Into the cool room full of women—
divorced, married, fertile, menopaused—
he drops his sizzling images

tongue nipple breast thrust

As his words gain velocity
the women's unison breathing slows.
They swallow their saliva
as in-con-spicu-ously as possible.

Crescendoing cries of climax

Their eyes lock on empty space,
carefully avoid other eyes.
Cheeks and lips neutrally flaccid.

Last panting parting stanza ends

Overly-casual they comment,
"Terrific!" "Great detail!"

Momentary satiated silence,
then—"Let's take a break."

Tightly clasped limbs unwind.
Thighs wobble toward the coffee pot.
Exhaled breath escapes in half-sobs.

Stunned into immobility Helen
brightly asks, "And what do you do
when you're not writing poetry?"

A STONING

There's gonna be a stonin'
a woman caught alone in
the very act of sinnin'.
What could she say?
They had stones in their hands.

Her only plea is,
certainly he is as guilty
as she is, and where is he?
What could they say?
They had stones in their hands.

They brought her to Jesus,
said, "See women tease us,
can't you just please us,
condemn her to death."
They had stones in their hands.

But Jesus spoke no word,
as if he had not heard,
he knelt on the hard earth
began to write.

Did he write their names,
uncover their shames?
What caused each man
to open his hand
and let the stones roll away,
let those stones roll away.

Let the stone roll away.

A GOOD SHEPHERD

A good shepherd is hard to find these days.

The job specs are uninviting:
Long days with only sheep for company.
No sick days, no overtime, no pension.
Must be able to find one sheep,
even if 99 are accounted for.
Must be able to rescue strays
from precipices and brambles.
Must be able to beat off wolves
or hungry human predators.

The terminology is confusing:
A sheep fold has nothing to do with origami.
Crooks and staff are not what you think!
Fleece is a negative word.
Laying down one's life for the sheep
is not an attractive advertising slogan.

The major problem lies with the sheep themselves.
Rams, ewes, lambs
do not want to be herded.
Each sheep an individual
with its own ovine rights,
anxious to follow its own path.
Not one willing to be a sacrificial lamb.

Yet, green pastures and still waters
do have a certain appeal.
No complaints from clients.
No boss looking over your shoulder.

All in all it's not a ba-a-ad job.

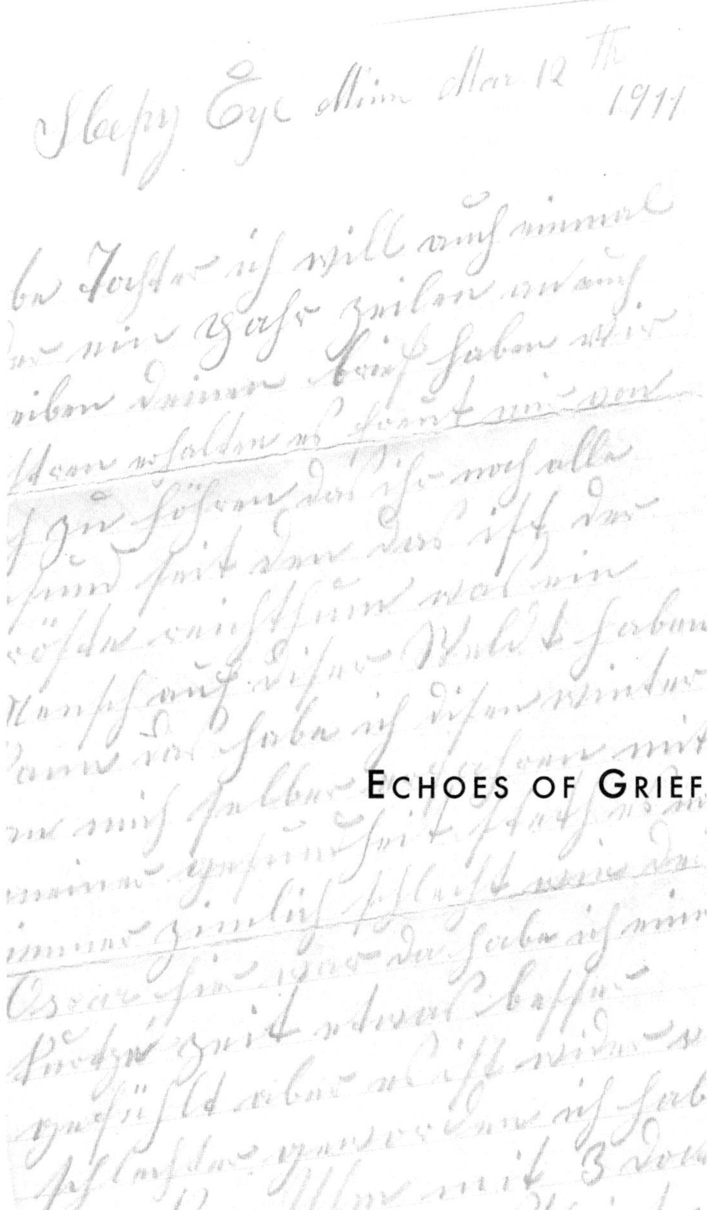
Sleepy Eye Minn Mar 12th 1911

Echoes of Grief

FRA PANDOLF REMINISCES

How fortunate for me,
commissioned to paint the Duchess.
Undoubtedly the Duke knows
my reputation, my credentials,
that I studied under Holbein.

The Duke pays well,
yes, better than well.'
And the Duchess is a jewel,
her skin tones translucent as pearl,
her eyes pale sapphire.

She sits, how shall I say,
as though my presence were a gift.
We do not speak, it would not be proper
to address her ladyship familiarly.

I watch her in the garden.
How kindly she speaks to the maid,
how merrily her laughter peals
as she gentles the white mule.

Only when the master enters
do I see a tremor move her hand,
her skin tinge gray.

Now the portrait is finished.
I place the oils into my case.
The Duke pays as agreed.
Yet, I sense he is not pleased.
Does he not see how her beauty shines?
How I captured the half-flush upon her throat.

ON PAPER SKIN

Lilac words loop lacy on the page,
as neat as folded hankies in a drawer
washed thin and soft, devoid of tears or rage,
still holding in their depths emotion's roar.
I open mother's diary, long dead,
I touch the page as though to stroke her face.
I trespass on her past with daughter's tread.
My fingers on her skin seek to retrace
the veins that tie me tightly to this life.
So young she left me growing up alone,
bereft of guidance when I was a wife,
I am mother, lacking mother of my bone.
   My heart still yearns for words of wise advice.
   Now words on yellowed paper must suffice.

Outsiders

Grandfather sailed into New York
on the *Bremerhaven* clutching the American dream.
He waved at the lady with the torch—
she was an immigrant too, from France.

He traveled to Minnesota,
where other Germans had settled.
The train traversed broad prairies.
Such good land, such opportunity.

A steamer trunk held his tools,
plane, lathe, chisels.
A cabinet maker by trade, also
undertaker, because he made coffins.

The day came when a farmer
hanged himself from barn rafters.
His widow pleaded with grandpa
to find a place to bury her husband.

Righteous townspeople would not
abide lying near a suicide.
They were buried south of town,
tidily laid down in order of death,
too thrifty to waste farm land on large plots.

A man must be put in the ground.
Grandpa walked north where a family
had a small private cemetery.
Could he buy a plot? Not *inside* the fence.

To this day, too sinful to lie
among neighbors,
that man lies alone   outside.

LETTER FROM HOME

Meine Liebe Tochter (my dear daughter)
Her father's words penciled on lined paper,
tremble in her fingers. She presses it to her cheek.
The postmark mockingly declares
that he is less than a train day away—
might as well be Egypt.

Her eyes search the long driveway
for her Oscar, gone to town to sell oats.
Will he return with a new letter?
Or whisky tales and empty pockets?

Scrawny chickens scratch hard dirt,
eating but laying no eggs in the heat.
Her eyes hunger for maple trees and creeks,
find only oceans of long grass,
surging, threatening her garden.

She wipes sweat on her flour sack apron,
stretches tiptoe, squints across the field
of durum wheat, hard as Dakota winters.
In the far corner, humps of two lilac bushes,
grow from roots she carried west
wrapped in burlap, cherished with water
Now they shade two marble lambs,
glittering white in the black-hot sun.

Folding the paper into her pocket
she turns her back to the taunting sky
and dust devil promises.

GRIEF HARD TO BEAR

My father buried his father-in-law twice.
The first time Oscar was laid down
in a family plot near the corner of a field.
He lay next to two babies too young to remember
and his first-born dead at nine of diphtheria
Then the 15 year-old, apple of his eye,
was lost to a blister turned to blood poisoning.
Something like that could drive a man to drink,
and it did, not that he didn't drink before,
but this was anesthesia, the waters of Lethe.

Granted he wasn't the best of husbands,
hauling grain to the elevator and spending
most of the day and the money in the pool hall.
In the haze of smoke and smell of beer
he played cards to forget Lena's accusing eyes,
forget the beautiful blue-eyed one.

The three little girls who survived
the diphtheria, after losing fingernails
and hair to high fevers, tugged at his pockets
looking for jawbreakers or peanuts.
He was almost afraid to touch them,
if he didn't know them too well
perhaps it wouldn't hurt as much.

His Lena never smiled anymore.
How could she love him,
this man who made babies destined to die.
Only the pool hall seemed safe from her eyes
and certainly God would not enter there.

At last his broken heart gave out
and he came to lie among his children,
out in the country by the farm
they once owned. Here daughter,
Elsie and family came each
Decoration Day to scythe
the long grass and plant flowers.

Now his Lena lived in town near Elsie,
her last remaining child of seven.
Aging she fretted about those graves
some miles away, looking shabby.
Soon she too would be exiled
to that forlorn burial plot.
She began a crusade to move bodies,
to re-plant those dear children
in a more appropriate, accessible plot.
Son-in-law John owned a grocery store.
Surely he could afford to move them.

She moaned, she wheedled, she whined
until he conceded and arranged
to have the long buried children
and more recently buried father-in-law
moved to the town cemetery, saving a spot
for Lena next to Oscar, a part of the deal
she wasn't too fond of, but she'd won the war.

When she died she had her children
surrounding her, she could put up with him,
after all, he didn't drink anymore.

And John was sometimes heard to say,
"Bet I'm the only man who paid
to have his father-in-law buried twice.

Conspiracy

I do not see them at first, the cows lying amid the tall tufts of a
Dingle peninsula pasture. They are not small, their hides not
camouflage-splotched. They are black and large. But I do not expect
to see them as they keep their cud-chewing faces cleverly positioned
behind the tufts, ridiculously believing, like the overweight lady in a
black swimsuit, that no one will notice. Of course, once I spot them,
they are as obvious as the spaghetti sauce on my husband's shirt. I
take a snapshot with my throw-away camera. Once developed it
takes several trips through the packet before I remember what I was
shooting. I point out the protruding bodies in the faraway pasture.
My friends nod and smile vaguely, wondering no doubt, what this
swat team of cows has to do with castle ruins and the lace-fringed
surf of Inch Beach. They do not take seriously this troop of guerrilla
cows hunkering, prepared for a surprise attack. But I am the spy who
has captured them on film. See there the horn missiles. There the
stealth steer. Be alert! Even now the cows are plotting. Even now the
stakes are high. Arm yourselves. Prepare for the slaughter!

DISTURBED

I know that voice hallooing at the door.
It wakens me from a lovely nap. Why
can't he let a guy rest? You know,
let sleeping dogs lie and all that rot.

Life is all priests and politics, death and taxes.
If I get up my sisters will find chores for me.
I want to lie here in cool darkness, forget
the demands, the turmoil, to rest my weary bones.

Now my good friend comes, raising his voice,
insisting that I rise, just when I am on the verge
of deepest sleep. Tangled in bedclothes
I stumble to the doorway, blinking.

Shading my eyes, I am surprised to find
a crowd gathered. People staring, stupefied.
What did they expect, when he called,
"Lazarus."

Intensive Care

He hides inside the coma
nourished through a nose tube,
fed drugs via IV threads,
air hose in his throat for breath,
a flesh robot beeping like an alien.

Our family takes turns entering
the guarded gates of ICU.
Our words find no connection.
We speak a language foreign
to his strange universe.
Yet, we call his name.

Stroking his arm,
we carefully place kisses
on islands of skin on his skull
between taped-on sensors.
We wait for his return
from some far planet.

At last there is a stirring.
Fever-chapped lips struggle
to deliver his urgent message.
I bend to hear him whisper,
"More kisses."

ORIENTATION

The boy noticed the left turn
as six black-suited men lifted
the casket from the horse-drawn coach.
Their heading was wrong, he thought.

My nine years old father,
fascinated by death's trappings
had witnessed many burials.
Often present for the digging of the grave,
he watched men shovel almost to China.

And he knew the rules.
All believers knew
on that Great Gettin' Up Mornin'
souls must stand up facing east,
leastwise in the Western Hemisphere,
leastwise in rural America.

Now he saw the mistake—
a coffin lowered wrong-way around—
the departed man going down
his feet to the west.

He pulled insistently at the preacher's sleeve.

The adults conferred.
This no small error,
too great a risk
to ignore the child.

Muscled arms grasped ropes,
raised the recently lowered casket,
opened the screwed down lid.
They viewed the dis-oriented body,
quickly turned and re-planted him,
restoring his resurrection hope.

And the mourners all said, "Amen."

HUNTING CLOUDS

Reclining in a duck blind
he pulls up a blanket
of cattails and reeds,
dreams of teenage hours,
the days of World War II
when returning heroes
walked the village streets,
when his long-legged father
loped through pheasant fields
teaching him how
to handle guns and life.

Now he hunts
with his own grown son,
escaping for a day or two
his wife's wheelchair.
He lays down the weight
of her illness, flees
to his prairie youth,
feeds on grass and sky.

October air tangy with freedom,
scudding clouds weightless.
A pair of Canada geese,
mated for life,
tilt into the wind,
glide toward his blind.
He cannot pull the trigger.

YOKED
"And the two shall become one flesh"

We slip into the yoke
in our dandelion days,
learn to walk the furrows
step on each other's feet.

So little we understand
the confines of this span,
abrasions on the shoulders,
concessions to gee and haw.

So little we understand
the length of dogged days
required to plow these fields,
to walk the furrows,
to plant a crop.

I learn to slow my step
to match your steady gait,
for the essence of a yoke
lies in facing forward,
two joined in purpose,
until the lulling tempo
erases thoughts of 'me'
and all is 'we.'

Somewhere ahead,
the unimaginable furrow
that must be plowed by one.

GRANDMA CANS CHICKENS

She stuffed whole chickens into bluegreen
2 quart jars, preserved them for long winters.
She stuffed grief to the bottom of her soul,
gnawed on it in the black nights.

She stitched together pieces of fabric,
intensely bent over her treadle machine,
sewing quilts to warm and cover
small bodies, no longer present.

Of the seven she birthed,
she buried six. Two she barely knew,
come and gone in days. Her dearest
first born reached 9 years of age
before diphtheria took her.

Grandma's lips seldom smiled,
pinched tightly shut. Holding in the hurt,
the questions. A change-of-life baby
seemed like another curse thrust upon her,
until this child proved to be a blessing,
conquering that armored heart,
She surrendered to love and hope.

As a teenager this child brightened the house
until a blister from new shoes,
turned into blood poisoning.
Her slow death destroyed all hope.

I played at grandma's feet near the treadle's
strong song. Sometimes I stayed the night,
climbed atop a mountain of freshly fluffed
feather tick, slid down the side, came to rest
against her old, lonely bones.

OLD PHOTO

My mother's shadow fills one corner
of the picture as she captures me
and a dog I no longer remember,
with her Kodak box camera.
My small face squints into the sun,
smile open and innocent.

If only I could rise, walk
into the arms of that mother
who died too young.
We would pick bachelor buttons.
She would read Grimm's Fairy Tales
while lying on my bed.
She would let me lick crystals
from the waxy Jello packet.

I am glad that little girl
did not know the shades of grief
that lay ahead. So many questions
not answered   not asked.
So many days lived in partial sun,
one corner a shadow of yearning.

Frogner Park, Oslo

We wander through the park
filled with Vigeland's naked people.
Sculpted square and sturdy,
rough granite Vikings:

man playfully tosses a child,
a woman on hands and knees crawls
across fjords and meadows,
her aging bosom sags,
a gray-fleshed boy-child stomps,
his face a fury of desires denied.

So unlike Michelangelo's David
we saw in Florence,
vainly displaying marbled muscles
and manhood white as Mediterranean sand.
Ready to step from his pedestal
to nibble grapes and olives,
to recline on an orgy of adoration.

While these stony Norwegians
forsake frivolity and pedestals
to pull herring from frigid waters,
grasp goat udders, make cheese.
Thrust long boats into strange seas,
plunge on to a new continent.

While an Italian in his stubby boat
takes credit for the discovery.

GALLOPING TOWARD NIGHT
For Robert Bly

Long caravans wandering across the page,
double-humped camels traversing oceans of sand
seeking oases rich with dates and Persian rugs.

Word pearls polished by desert sand.
A wind blowing through us. Who is knocking?
Sentences of joy a thousand years long.

Robert, hold on to the reins.
Do not fall off. We cry out. Hold on Robert,
as your horse gallops toward night.

ABOUT THE AUTHOR

DORIS LUETH STENGEL, a retired schoolteacher, lives in Brainerd, Minnesota. She is past president of the League of Minnesota Poets and the National Federation of State Poetry Societies (NFSPS). She has poetry and articles published in journals, magazines, and anthologies including *Encore, Dust & Fire, Talking Stick, Lake Country Journal, Her Voice, County Lines, On and Off the Wall,* and *Moon Reader.* Her chapbook SMALL TOWN LINES was published by Finishing Line Press, Georgetown, Kentucky in July 2012.

Contact
Doris Lueth Stengel
1510 S 7th Street
Brainerd, MN 56401
218-829-9072
dpoet@brainerd.net